Seasons and Creatures

Seasons and Creatures

Lauris Edmond

Auckland
Oxford University Press
Oxford New York

Oxford University Press
Oxford   New York   Toronto
Delhi   Bombay   Calcutta   Madras   Karachi
Petaling Jaya   Singapore   Hong Kong   Tokyo
Nairobi   Dar es Salaam   Cape Town
Melbourne   Auckland
and associated companies in
Beirut   Berlin   Ibadan   Nicosia

Oxford is a trade mark of Oxford University Press

First published in 1986
© Lauris Edmond 1986
Reprinted 1987, 1988

Acknowledgements:
Acknowledgements are due to the editors of the following publications,
in which some of these poems have appeared:
Landfall, More Magazine, and the *New Zealand Listener* in New Zealand; the
Canberra Times, Mattoid, and *Westerly* in Australia; and the *Honest Ulsterman,
Planet, PN Review, Poetry Now, Stand,* and *Verse* in the United Kingdom. Some
poems have also been broadcast on the Concert Programme of Radio New
Zealand, and by the BBC.

The assistance of the New Zealand Literary Fund is gratefully acknowledged.

ISBN 0 19 558159 8

Cover designed by Fay McAlpine
Photoset in Palatino by Jacobsons
and printed in Hong Kong
Published by Oxford University Press
5 Ramsgate Street, Auckland 5, New Zealand

Contents

III: Time Future

For Tess

Human Voice

Stone and star do not force their music on us,
flowers are silent, things hold something back,
because of us, animals deny
their own harmony of innocence and stealth,
the wind has always its chastity of simple gesture
and what song is only the mute birds know,
to whom you tossed an unthreshed sheaf on Christmas Eve.

To be is enough for them and that is beyond words. But we,
we are afraid not only in the dark,
even in the abundant light
we do not see our neighbour
and desperate for exorcism
cry out in terror: 'Are you there? Speak!'

Vladimir Holan
Translated by Jarmila and Ian Milner

I: Rain in the Hills

From the south

An orange flare of montbretia
briefly blazes by a fence
leaping past the car here,
and some duller embers beyond —
bracken I think — static, unconsuming
fevers that lightly enter the blood
as it courses in larger directions.

I am not even quite sure if that's
what they were, Monkey's Britches,
shoddy plebeians with bright lips
incurably parted, multiplying as they do
with indecent aplomb
on skinny verges, bulbs broad-bottomed
and hairy all over
cramming the dust down below —

and anyway they have vanished. Yet
they remind me, those public
fandangos, that our longings are themselves
a kind of happiness, a quick tilt
of attention at a spark obliquely caught
like a flash in the sun at a moving window,
glimpse of some passionate uncertainty
which is what we call daily living in these
nervous, unfinished, beautiful islands.

The outside room

It was the moon poised with a bright patience
low over the paddocks, the silence standing
about in surprise as though newly arrived,
the constant soft bleat of the sheep
and the earth, most of all the earth itself

sending up its unaccountably tender emanations
and winy smell, telling me what dew can do
to sap-heavy grass and sheep shit, and
to the sheep too, obscurely coiled
in the oily emollients of their wool —

all this, as I crept out in the no-time
after midnight, going to pee by the fence
squatting in the cool heady freshness, night's
elbow flung over the hill and the strange
spare light of the stars beyond —

all whispering, explaining, declaring
that the persecuted earth has not yet
resigned its ancient romance with seasons
and creatures; and so clearly my body
couldn't help exulting as it tiptoed back

over the cold crush of the grass, stones
by the door, and I saw without looking the dark window
behind which the young lay asleep together
holding once again safe until morning
their dream of a lifetime to come.

Rain in the hills

The dead stay with you always
taking house-room, finding in you
their haven and harbour; and this happens
even though you know their going sealed off
for you a segment of the whole circle
of things and now wherever you walk there is
some part of the hills and sky
you do not see, though it is not
obscured by the seasons or weather:

but where you are, in this impaired place,
they also remain and are necessary
and beautiful as the thundery light
over the black spurs on an evening
of spring rain; and being there
they will change, not as images
of yourself but in their own way,
allowing you to perceive them
with a fresh vision again and again.

Even the terrible deaths you believed
would shrink your heart forever
do not come to an end or leave you,
for you cannot repudiate your suffering
— it is in you, it is what you have become:
the limited world of loss is still
your support, your delight, and as real
as this hill angled with black stone
and the violet clouds above it —

they are yours, stately and strange
as they are, holding your defeat
and your knowledge of defeat, which is also
entirely at home in you, in how you
watch and speak, in your composition,
your nerve pathways, your membranes
and cells. This is the chemistry of pain.

The Noh plays

'Three months,' they said in July
but it is November and you are here still
gaunt on the pillow, your eyes
following us, pleading not so much for us
to settle your question but to know
how a man might give up his asking.

For us too the time is defined —
this is the last act: we cannot afford
a single careless gesture.
In your room at given positions
we are poised in a watchful patience.
The white window dare not close its eye.

In the Noh plays of Japan death is not
mentioned, but a character speaks
as a ghost bearing the soul of a man
— one who has endured his torment
in the Three Worlds of nature
and earned his release;

he plays out his suffering, his folly,
his search for wisdom; at last
his voice dims. Out of the silence
a young man begins to recount
new and remarkable exploits. But these are
the first words of another cycle.

Orthopaedic ward

With you in these clean rooms
are the secret creatures
'living in millions'
as Sister observes
'in your mouth, ears,
nostrils'; disporting themselves no doubt
in the lush spongy jungles
of everyone's hair:

a below-stairs society
settled in blind unicellular hierarchies
manifesting its potency
with the greatest indifference
— no question but living's
for staying alive, and killing
as necessary and plain
as hospital pyjamas — a truth

we are learning here
among trolleys of folded linen
stacked crutches, wounds
swelling with newly invented species,
the spectre of amputation
stalking the corridor after lights out.
'Good luck for yours,' says our jovial anguish
as each trolley trundles off

to another trial by oblivion
and we put an ear to the wall
as though we could pick up the murmur
of hordes that can simply increase
till they help themselves
to everything that we are —
barbarians silently massing
at the gate of the matchless city.

The lecture

I am just going downstairs to where
I shall tell them lies. Up here
at the window the maple trees' shadow

fingers the indigo dusk and the fireflies
carry their tiny cargoes of light
up, down, right to the ground, then

almost over the high branches again
riding their currents of bark-scented dark
with an unquestioning poise

giving off sparks from a wholesome
summer travail. I could watch them
all night; what I cannot do

is burn at the small purifying fires
of their industry. I shall go soon,
persons are waiting to hear what I claim

that I know. I will talk down, say
'in respect of', offer insights, despising
both them and myself, but thinking:

'Up there in the quiet room
where the fireflies are to be seen
at work in their luminous trees

there is my truth, my candour, my courage,
there I too can shine with the natural
intermittent light of myself,'

— and then I shall go on holding forth.

Cows

I followed the by-pass road behind Woodville
the sky as clean as a cut apple
around me the milky and putrid smell of cows
— in the rise of the dew, cows steaming
and wandering, slung from their frames
like black and white blankets
hung out to dry. They do say
you can make milk from grass, without cows
and their warm galumphing machinery
and tunnelly stomachs . . . Bah! at the thought
steam bursts in an angry spiral
straight up from a cake of shit
and the small ears twitch and shudder
above the luminous heads.

Or so I say. But these are the real,
the solid cows that cannot quarrel
or kill, have never fallen in love
and could not defend the dumb expertise
of their milk-making, which they did not invent
and do not observe with the least interest,
any more than they remember in autumn
how they roared all night in the spring
when their calves were taken away.

They do not suppose this matters,
nor that anything else does — indeed,
they do not suppose. Their time is entirely
taken up with the delicious excruciating
digestion of existence
and if they please me on the by-pass road
in the ripening sun this morning
that is wholly my affair.

Near Hunterville: wheat

Nothing but gold
white straw gold
dry wine, old
gold of fulfilment
past effort past lust
past even indolence
stalks drawn to a fine
brittle marrow
full heads barely touching
their pillows of heat

red threshing machine
looming and still
on a colourless sky
farm hand whistling
unhurried, assured
the readiness
reaching
each bright atom of air
the drawn breath —
the death.

On the road to Ballarat

Her face shone while she talked, very fast,
leading us in from the car
'It's bluestone, 1830s I think,' and showed
how the architect had devised
a new mezzanine floor
without changing the attic bedrooms.

When she stopped the quiet grew huge
in the parlour, with its white plates
patterned with ships, standing in rows
on the grandmotherly dresser
and the fringed rug, hand-woven
and slightly askew. We leaned near
the fire. Would they ever go back
to Kansas? 'It's lonely here,' she said
to the far fields lying at the window
featureless as a prairie. He came in then

austerely friendly, like a preacher,
and changed his boots by the door; she cut
slices of cornbread, looking towards him
with a kind of surprise, as though each day
had this same shy way of putting itself together.
In the end Australia was too big and silent;
they pulled up like an anchor
the great furniture, the Mayflower plates,
and slowly sailed for home.

O.E.*

You listen, grieving, to Schubert's
Unfinished Symphony on an evening
already haunted by pinched crowds
in Earl's Court Road this morning

veined leaves of the *caladium hortulamus*
(the label declares) open towards you
from a pot on the marble table, as though
to reveal a peculiar history (Schubert

it is said could not finish the work
having heard that fatal summer the news
of his syphilis) and there is
fruit on a square plate, one peach,

four red nectarines, perfect still life.
Earlier, in the underground, a train
curved sharply towards your window,
veered away while you gasped, drew back

as if hit by it: traveller, you are making up
your realities. These are the profiles
of somebody else's inventions, cast
like shadows in the empty room of your days.

* *'Overseas experience'*

The ghost moth

Once we lived so close to the bush
each day wore the beech trees' rangy profile,
all night the creek purred, brushing
the antennae of our sleep; in the evening
moths came pouring into the lamplight,
some small, blue-sheened, as though it was
light itself combed to dust on their wings

or a ghost moth stared from the doorway
sheathed in its gentle shallow gaze;
and we ourselves seemed diffused like
the light, and would wander away
past the moths to the leaf-shivering trees
as though summoned in secret
by the morepork's comfortless cry.

That earthy unearthly life is over now
but sometimes still when you come in
from the purposeful street and hesitate,
blinking, I think of the moths
how they wheeled into the lamp's bright
aureole and turned and turned, dazzled
by something they never really saw.

Early afternoon in the lounge bar

Over the last half of draught you observed
'He's got HITLER on his T-shirt.' I
walking past asked could we perhaps —
did he mind — under his jacket (now covering
that apparently controversial torso)?

'It is, actually,' his artless Australian smile
had no trouble telling us. 'Look — '
HITLER EUROPEAN TOUR 1939-45, there it was
printed on white cotton-knit stretched
over the carelessly athletic chest.

The three of us grinned, a good moment.
It's bloody old history doing it, I thought,
my God, just that — there's a global grief
the disgrace of a nation
relentlessly breeding disgrace

and forty years on someone too young to remember
is being silly about it. O life O continuity
I thought, to be so slyly alive
at lunch time in the lounge bar
of the dingy old Cock and Bull.

An orange cat

Come into the little wooden towns
walk with me, covertly watched
by for instance Mrs McGrath in the dairy
and Walter O'Connor dreaming his luck
on the TAB's peeling old seat,
wander the road a mile wide
to Major and Major Solicitors
unseen behind the dim frosted square
of their window, last painted in 1949

see where the poplars are greening
alongside the camping ground
and the white wooden church standing
drier than Danny O'Dowd
before the bar opens up at eleven —

dry too the ancient verandahs
shrunk by a century's seasons
on cottages built when the plain was a forest
the towns no more than depots
for horses and men at large on a wooded island
twelve thousand miles from home;

it was all trees, it was timber
and timber it still is,
and the sweet slummocky smell of the sun
on doorways and porches, Sally McCutcheon
in grey perm and a cardigan
getting along in her slippers,
Mick Griffin rolling his own at the entrance
to *Saddlery All Leather Goods Ltd*
and an orange cat lazily limbering up
on the other side of the road.

Exodus

All over the autumn counties
the thistledowns are flying
the Bastard Scotch and Slender Winged Thistle
Californian Heraldic
and the Plumeless Yellow Star

each taking off in a high sigh of wind
to ride over the soft rolls of hay
and scattered silage
the white goats at their angular munching;

there goes the Blessed Thistle, once used
to cure gout, the Creeper
with wings to its down and a parachute
of fine hairs, Sow Thistle
and the small Melancholy, dusty
and faint in its flight —

I watch them go with a kind of grieving,
a perverse sadness that lingers
on the indistinct margin of late afternoon
as though it is here that our seasons are ending
and these seeds passing over
the harvested farms are the last
of our reign as planters, destroyers,
before we too are tossed from
the plundered misunderstood kingdom.

II: The Process

The sums

Somewhere you are always going home;
some shred of the rag of events
is forever being torn off and kept
in an inside pocket or creased satchel
like the crayon drawing, blurred now,
you frowned over once in a desk:

it's kept for the moment when you go
mooching along the verandah and through
the back door, brass-handled, always ajar,
to where the floured apron stands monumental
above veined legs in a cloud of savoury steam,
mince, onions, the smell of childhood's Julys;

there again you are quick-flounced and shrill
shrieking on a high stool the answers
to sums — multiplication, addition, subtraction,
all the mysteries known as 'Mental' — alchemy
that could transmute 48 + 17 (when you got it,
yelling) to a burst of fire in the blood —

it is still there, still finding its
incorruptible useless answers,
your life's ruined verandah, the apron,
the disfigured legs that with a stolid
magnificence used to hold up the world.

Tempo

In the first month I think
it's a drop in a spider web's
necklace of dew

at the second a hazel-nut; after,
a slim Black-eyed Susan demurely folded
asleep on a cloudy day

then a bush-baby silent as sap
in a jacaranda tree, but blinking
with mischief

at five months it's an almost-caught
flounder flapping back
to the glorious water

six, it's a song
with a chorus of basses: seven, five grapefruit
in a mesh bag that bounces on the hip
on a hot morning down at the shops

a water-melon next — green oval
of pink flesh and black seeds, ripe
waiting to be split by the knife

nine months it goes faster, it's a bicycle
pedalling for life over paddocks
of sun
no, a money-box filled with silver half-crowns
a sunflower following the clock
with its wide-open grin
a storm in the mountains, spinning rocks
down to the beech trees
three hundred feet below
— old outrageous Queen Bess's best dress
starched ruff and opulent tent of a skirt
packed with ruffles and lace
no no, I've remembered, it's a map
of intricate distinctions

purples for high ground burnt umber
for foothills green for the plains
and the staggering blue
of the ocean beyond
waiting and waiting and
aching
with waiting

no more alternatives! Suddenly now
you can see my small bag of eternity
pattern of power
my ace my adventure
my sweet-smelling atom
my planet, my grain of miraculous dust
my green leaf, my feather
my lily my lark
look at her, angels —
this is my daughter.

The capable spirit

Oh yes happiness arrives all right,
it set itself up here last Friday
adopting like Maui all necessary forms
to suit the present adventure

chattering in the weatherboards
of a lean-to kitchen, rustling like paper
in tacked bright prints on the walls
gloating over our shoulders
at these complete little feet
faint-stroked eyebrows
half-cat's-eye pale shell fingernails
unfocused blue eyes;

try animal, mineral, vegetable, this is
the most various magic any of us will know;
in a bedscape of milky breast
it moons and whispers, goes to perch
on a yellow bucket in the bathroom

rash phantom pretending to command
all the great ceremonies in this one;
and it does seem just now, in this flimsy cottage,
it can do anything. Clever with love,
it is busy composing a life.

In the grain

Watch me: I am a spider
industrious and clever, the eye
of my instinct bright,
I can tell you of porridge and quarrels
I do not ruminate.
I know matai wood smokes in the stove
manuka too; maire is grey and dense
and burns like coal.
I am adroit with the iron lids
that cover the flame
while considering serious questions
'What is a ghost?' 'Is dead a place?'

Pregnant I was sleepy and fractious
remembered my iron and calcium tablets
did not smoke; when a child is learning
to read I examine symbols
together we frown at a page where
he writes with a fierce
and scrupulous pressure — runes on a rock
scratched at a world's beginning
a web pegged out on a fence
making diamonds of dew.

Time stretches and thickens
I discover boys' pants are shorter
and tighter this year; by lamplight
I read of the Heffalump . . .
I am spider, silkworm, magpie
my nest full of glittering accidental
treasures. I neither ask nor judge
I tell, I guess, I take note —
there are storm clouds over the mountain?
bitterness in another house? news from the south?
I have no time to look, to wonder
beyond the enduring confusion.

The world waits at the door
while a child ties her laces for school.
Do not pity me. This
is a dense sufficiency.

Neighbours

Earthquake. It split the universe open
the red roof fell on the ground, bricks
simmered and burst — a shock beyond
all fear, all surprise. Earthquake: I'd
never heard the word but I remember
a black shimmer of sunlight, the sharp
dry grass, our inexplicable tumbling
the turning to see that wild scarlet
smoke, our school, not twenty feet away.

Three were killed in the violent dust
one who had lived next door, my daily
companion, the friend with whom I
dawdled the green osier tunnels along
our road, splashed in the river shallows
gorged in the plum tree that spanned
the spiky hedge between his house and mine.
I remember a freckled face, intent
and solemn. His name was Billy Pollock.

Hymns Ancient and Modern

On a rough night spinning past
the macrocarpas' violent shadows
wind wrenched the car sideways
till for very apprehension I began singing
the purposeful hymns of childhood
All Hail the Power   O Worship the King
Su-un of my So-oul Thou Sa-aviour Dear

mist sent its wraiths whirling
queerly over the farms as I intoned
Rock of Ages, even at last Lest We Forget
(oh the smell of chrysanthemums
on terrible Anzac Days!).

But truly on Tinakori Hill
the dark spurs motioned me past
and I came on home. Up steps to the windy door
key in the lock   the first light switch
mail in a pile on the table
your letter.

'It happened last week, in England.
The children have been told.'
Six-year-old Josie, died of a brain tumour.
A small child, pretty, inclined to giggle
— that's really all I know.
How silent the wind is
it has no voice now
no song. It is just wind, after all
just air
the cruel and stupid air that will always
come and go at random —

in All Saints Sunday School
at a death we sang Abide With Me
in our effortless thin voices

and looked out the window
savouring all the Sunday dinners
still to come.

Mortimer

Mornings first and naturally
were milk and Mortimer: six o'clock
he banged his bike against the shed, neatly
lifted the billy off — he kept a hook
tied to the handlebars, a boy's love
for contraptions still at twenty-five

— or so they said he was. Each day early in
the kitchen, I fed my teenage greed
for reading, huddled beside the thin
flame, all in impatience I could
drag from the ancient stove. 'Wants air,'
he said, and gave it breath to leap and flare

and hung around a while, but didn't dare
say more than 'Good yarn eh?' or 'How's yer Dad?'
grinning his ugly friendly grin. There
on my fifteenth birthday so he awfully stood
smelling of milking, sweaty from the ride,
and lurched towards me — queerly afraid

of harmless Mortimer, I dumped the book
and ran and hid until I heard his tyres
crunch the gravel, then breathed and wandered back
and gazed, alert in the subsiding of my fears,
at the scent bottle, the adorable tiny globe for spray
— till sick with childishness I turned away.

Presences

Thinking this morning of Susan
mourning my dead friend
remembering a sharp smiling despair
when her lungs denied her breath
to laugh or speak

my mind admits another visitor
who in the same week
lay on my kitchen table
thrusting tiny legs
as though to kick holes in this
quotidian eternity; his fingers gripped
whatever scrap the vasty world held out

and when he cried we ran to offer him
an eager solicitude, as though we knew
breath merely slept in her
and love is all it needs to wake
and start its work again.

The process

In a time of desolation
to recall the rich acres of summer
is to know you are alone; the others
have gone, or changed irrecoverably —

it is as though change itself
is the auctioneer who put under the hammer
a precious expanse, knocking it down
to the bead-bright eyes of loss, illness
separation, death —

so we no longer lean on our elbows
at Frank's narrow table, his trout mornay
steaming under the lifted spoon
nor sprawl in the study
where poems burgeoned and broke
against Mexican embroideries,
Meg stumbling over our legs as she
ran out, weeping, and Vincent spoke
of white horses in a manic moonlight
somewhere in the Cotswolds — while all the time

outside lay love's precarious landscape
ours without act of possession
the place that, as we talked,
time had already noted yard by silent yard
and marked for sale by dissolution.

A reckoning

You were my friend, accomplice in
the copious plotting parents are a party to;
through centuries of jovial boredom
on the beach we stuck it out together

then separately awake hallucinated
over teenage accidents in cars, until
a door at last breathed out and cracks
of guilty silence shot us dead asleep.

Our fears kept us close; pride too,
and the small events' unmerciful momentum.
It was a walled garden, safe to quarrel in,
love coming down on us reliably as rain.

We were its keepers, so intent we did not see
the change of sky, the gradual departures
— then there was just a man, a woman
slamming some old gate on a quiet plot

ill-tempered without learnt weather
and the rule of law. Who were
the guardians then, and who, despite
that virtuous authority, the guarded?

Photograph

A young woman, head poised on a long neck,
contemplates a vase of white roses — thus,
sixty years ago, a lady's image. I watch

as though any minute she'll wake up
in that shaded parlour, shrug with the old
ironic impatience and laugh 'Who, me?

A smudge on a scrap of paper treated
with chemicals — you can settle for that?'
Mother, you're ten years dead. The quiet

silting covers everything in the end
— the bitter stoop of your shoulders
as you fought for each breath, furious,

the days bleeding away in secret
out of the emptying lungs; you, young
under the osier tree, so blown about

by laughter you could hardly stand; we three
doubled up too by your lunatic fancies;
the hot grass, burnt sky of summer, bright

ephemeral universe that moves, changes
and allows me at last simply to hold what I have:
white dress, six formal flowers, coiled hair

fingers enclosing a slender vase, still,
desperate; that I remember how it was always
to last for ever — the moment; the love.

Penalties

Your strength is a terrible sentence.
Everywhere you look there are gifts
received by the weak. She is sorrowing;
she mourns till his heart breaks, she
will never be his, but that yearning
will fire a hundred passionate
declarations. To grow strong is
to stand alone, at a window perhaps,
watching the sunset as it stains
the hills, to busy yourself with
your complex comprehension.
How distant, like a country
you travelled years and years before,
is that open place waiting
like washed sand for a new footprint,
how purely it took the mark
of his coming, how it could conceive
of no other pressure but lay perfect,
the virgin flesh you believed
would never have to bleed.

Winter morning

Now I can stand, walk, open my mouth
and speak — but inch by inch
slowed by the cruel grip of my skin;

I will walk carefully to the city
not looking at your image in the bleak sea
whipped by the southerly wind;

when the small shops open for newspapers
and tobacco I will pass among strangers
exchanging strictly formal greetings

— tell me, do you not feel it? Do you not know?
Without our love we are nothing; we are
naked and the icy weather will destroy us.

At the hospital

I thought him much older, a gentleman
of style, neat black moustache, debonair
hand waving across the corridor

from his cotton-quilt corner to mine;
the fluffy girl who stayed so long by his bed
reading as though at home must be his daughter.

'Got it all sussed out,' he'd call
over the breakfast trays, his legs
a white mountain hiding the strict machinations

of surgeons, 'told the boss I'll do
his job lying down, lucky bastard he is . . .'
and at once he was young, just a boy.

'Twenty-one,' murmured the girl, bringing
us all ripe peaches, 'his brother's a haemophiliac
too,' and we understood how each act

could touch off the treacherous bleeding. Days
they prepared him for theatre drawn curtains
kept everyone quiet; I considered

my own wound, superficial, properly healing;
he began to look further away
and the waving grew smaller. On the last day

I gave him my macadamia nuts. 'You'll be fine,'
and he grinned, jaunty like his own boss,
like an uncle, like anyone living for ever —

I walked quickly, but it was a hard mile
to the big double doors at the corner
and Sister, nodding and smiling goodbye.

Epithalamion

for L.E.R.

Wife, woman, hausfrau, female companion
you are rightly summoned again
to the careful ceremony. But you know,
you never left off being married
as you went on guarding your supplies
(ripening figs, soup stock, pears
to be bottled) with a gentle managing tact
somehow avoiding the crowd of waiting
ambitions while you nourished the cells
of the house — a grandchild's teddy bear
the failing lassiandra bushes . . .

wife, wif, woman, let me re-define the notion
stand it before me, observe
the natural wave of its greying hair
the unclamorous refrain of the voice
and the confident smell of a cleaned kitchen
the labelled jars glinting, a whiff
of cut grass at the window —

yes the wife in you, widowed, kept up
its daily preparation of house room
for the heart, stayed mysteriously content
with the ancient humilities
a lit fire, a boiling kettle
the deep solace of bread.

III: *Time Future*

Still

On December evenings you walk into the house
quite simply, smiling inwardly as you did,
a nearly nonchalant ghost

choosing — for you have more choice
than I'd have supposed — those
fading gold six o'clocks

we wandered through to sit
on the balcony, narrow and gritty
as it was; and took in

the complicated scents of the gum tree
and were washed by the light
of a mellow impermanent sky.

Coming through

Beautiful woman laughing
throat quivering in this smudgy light
back arching, the tide of delight
rising in you like a transfusion;
your breasts ripple like blown grass
— the good one, and the other
made of scars and contraptions —

you never laughed like this before,
taken over, lost in it (there are tears
on your face): you're adrift now
each day's a fresh notice
that your moorings have been untied
and you're out on the swell

you can take any direction:
now your maimed body has given up planning
it's abandoned
to its narrow, blue-green, lace-flounced
elegant incomplete present —

next time I must make an appointment
I have to take my chances;
in your understood freedom
you are already
half out of sight.

Camellias

1: *Femme de lettres*

Today was small and precious
each ellipse of sunlight
sidling across your hair
and eyebrows, the beard you tug
between other grander gestures;

the glossed camellia leaves
stood still, poised as though to be
the more exquisitely excluded
along with the pale petals we did not
notice as intently we leaned and talked

each word brighter-bodied for
the shadow of the ones we did not say
— this is after all the edited life
to cut, to prune, select, is my profession
— I did not know such practice

could command a lazy room of polished leaves
and sun. Even your kiss ached
with a sweet forfeited knowledge;
behind us waited those still, crisp stalks,
the flowers a single breath can tarnish.

Camellias

2: Working

A rough morning, wind thumping the house
and all about it these bustling bodies
shoulders sawing up sunlight in chunks
hands scrabbling and beating the clay
of my lumpy hillside; three young men
I have asked to conceive it as garden
their flung shouts whirling
along corridors of the wind.

Older, I stay inside (besides, I am
paying) here where camellias are stuck
in a pot and Wilhelmina, young too
and inextinguishably cheerful, is cleaning
my windows. What a season is spring —
raw, hyperactive, blatantly kind
reeking like sweat of the future:
did I too once take the season full on

like a fist, like a kiss, like
a drowning . . . ? Look, the flowers
have fallen, they lie like pink
crumpled skin on the floor, but the leaves,
the unyielding bright leaves, are
making a stand. I likewise turn back
to my desk, to this page, to you,
to hear how my poem tells you.

After dark

There was some pain, but afterwards
I slept; and then my body found itself,
grew warm, flirtatious even, left
to open the door to an austere stranger:
'Charming, my dear,' he stepped inside,

'your skirt's alluring swing, gestures
of comprehension, style . . . but, you know,
these things do not matter now; I want
instead what all of this conceals —

I desire your very flesh, so keenly
I shall peel it from the bone, your eyes
I'll close, your mouth silence with my kiss:
you will in turn receive the one entire,
absolute possession.' Then he left.

My body found his card and took it up
but quickly put it down; the object was
unpleasant, strangely textured,
harsh and wordless; black.

He had already said he'd call again.

Dunedin in July

After fifty the mind's muscles begin to
slacken, the view it encompasses grows
broader, yet I think more lightly held.

This morning on a cold Otago hillside
I take in Mount Cargill, snow beard
untrimmed, the spires of sober churches,

the steely light of the sky, near me
in black earth under the ngaio tree
a single snowdrop two inches high;

and in the same moment, precisely set
in its narrower frame, the same hill sprinkled
with beech tree shadow in summer

a young woman walking and watching
beginning thirty years ago to learn
all I have inescapably become.

She is quiet and merry and spry, secure
in the power she has no idea
she will lose or relinquish repeatedly

in the anguish of later seasons —
she is so close I can almost touch her
nearly smile into those unseeing green eyes;

behind her the hills and the city
tilt and steady in the piercing southern light
as though to confer the outline

of one horizon on older and more confused,
more hurtful angles. Standing here
I can just smell the scent of that flower.

Purple irises

Look at them, at the adroit
the ingenious, the cock-eyed
symmetry of the things —
the unexpected answer
to an unfathomable equation
each wayward
stroke
composing
a lop-sided harmony:

they settled briefly
like tropical butterflies
in my stolid bedroom
having flown in with the dawn
rioting high, describing
intricate figures above the kowhai
and early jasmine
then swooped to perch
alert
and set
with amusing skill their violet wings
on these severe stalks

now arching their bodies
the aristocrats
they glance at me with quick
condescension: sickness
they say
is a peasant.

A note

Our debt to time is never-ending; all,
all has been exacted in the erosion of that
high astonishment we knew when — do you

remember? — we came suddenly upon each other
in the street and stood not touching, skeined
together in the profound embrace we understood

we could not have, living it up
in the heady metropolis our imagined map
of nature showed was ours. Well, we live there

now, citizens of each other, familiar
to the very stones we walk upon, no longer
caring if a crowd appears, the private place

being anybody's now, ours after all a common
contract, deep, incurious. Your outline of me
stays the same through all my changing,

mine of you is scarred by lazy habitual lies.
The sun sets each day upon the shadows
we've become; what the times ask of us, we are.

Myopic, forgetful, adrift about this
tarnished landscape, I pause
and turn; salute your constancy.

Time future

What have I done with the future?
Why does it torment me,
the whiff I receive
from the small snowball flowers
in this twilit garden?

Eager with spring they whisper
of an unimaginable tomorrow
I have somewhere set aside
so it hurts with a sudden sharpness
this breath of the earth

travelling in wonder, unprotected,
its sweet ignorance fluttering like moths
in the dusk; my heart
is a small field sown
with old yearnings. Go on, go on

it's not me walking here fast
on the pavement, it is you,
young white tree of the soft balls
of desire — you are the mover, the flyer.
I am the one standing still.

The invasion

So this is what it is like —
nothing here, where I live,
but news from a distance
coming like a report from the front
of the ravages of action
to those appalled at base.

I have no power to re-deploy
that innocent violence
— it is hard enough to believe in it —
skin like an old pullover
dragged over the head, crumpled
in scornful caricature
of a lifetime of moods
breasts meek as a boy's, mocking
their vanished opulence, bones taut
in a thinning garment of flesh

— it's a disguise cast in derision
a badly managed facsimile
spurious in its authority. I am
a country divided, taken over
by the invader, bounded by
insulting frontiers.

Yet I have my Resistance
my government in exile
a cabal of one to fight my
undercover battles; no one can
stop me giving the orders. In here
I shall fight my life to the death.